I0486600

Distortions of Heroes

This is our title page and copyright page. Don't freak out.

Juan's Instagram: juanfmuro
Email: studiojaone@yahoo.com
Jon's Instagram: castanedajon
Email: elsapoman@yahoo.com

Special thanks to Vivi, Babs, and Emma

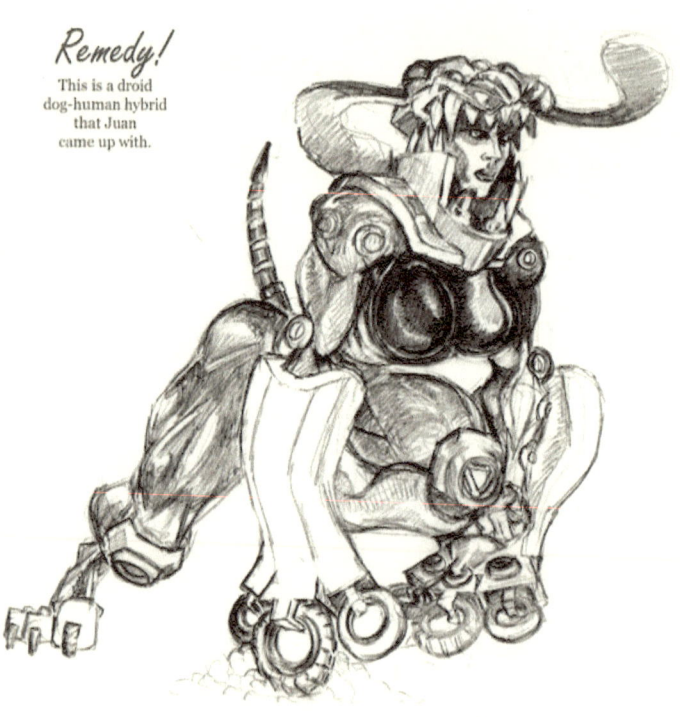

Remedy!

This is a droid
dog-human hybrid
that Juan
came up with.

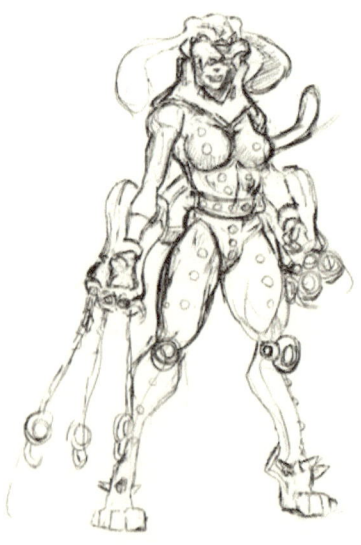

Original Remedy Sketch

Pheral

He's feral, ferocious, and ready to chew on your bones.

Douse yourself in soy sauce for a quick death!

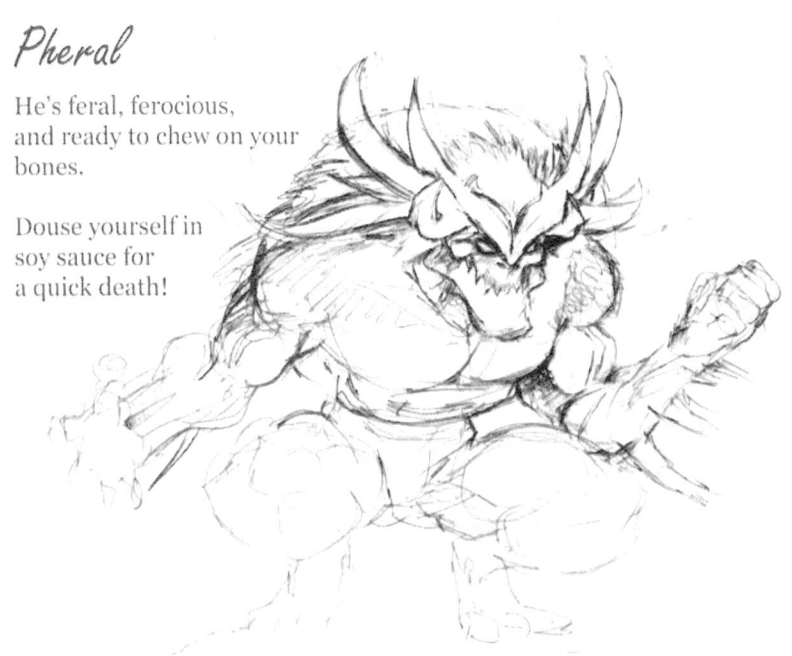

Pheral

Monstrosity

In perpetual dark

Hide in inky shadow

Snarling like grinding rocks

Hides in trees

Fear inducer

Dream killer

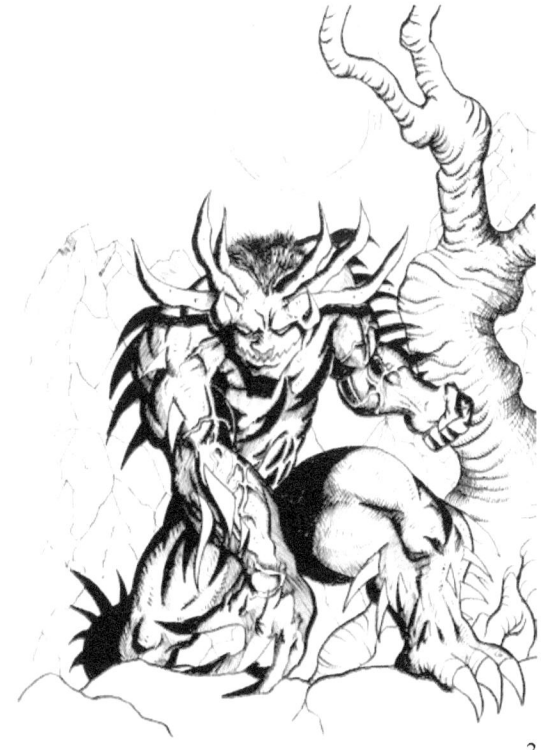

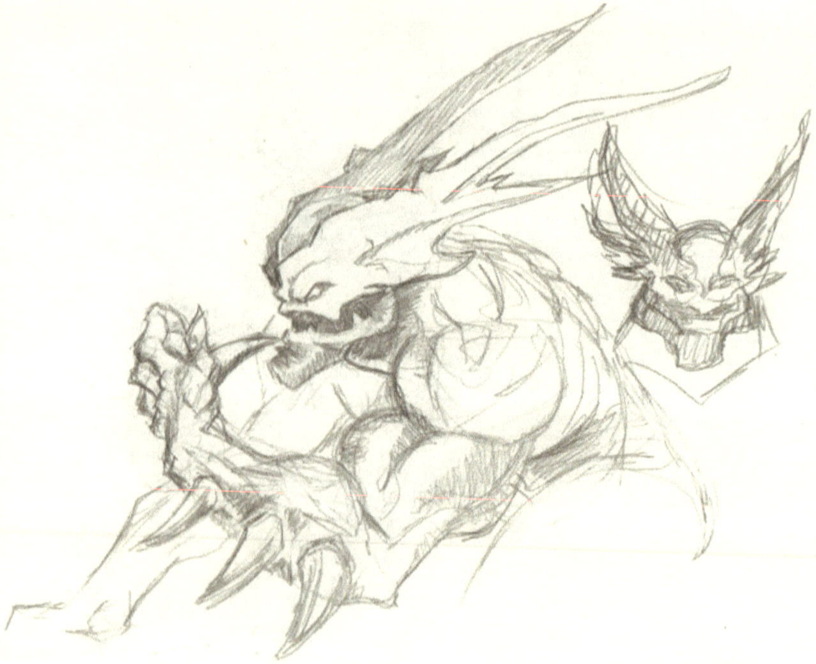

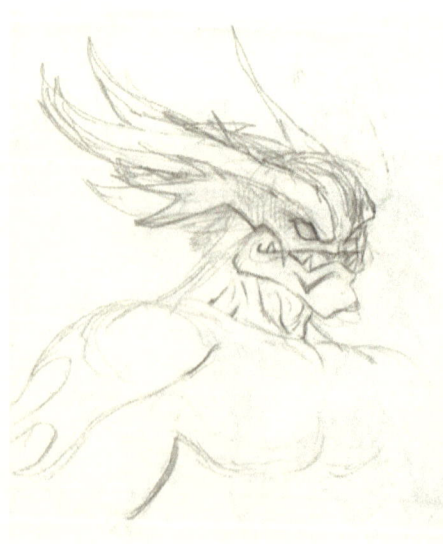

4

Deathpool

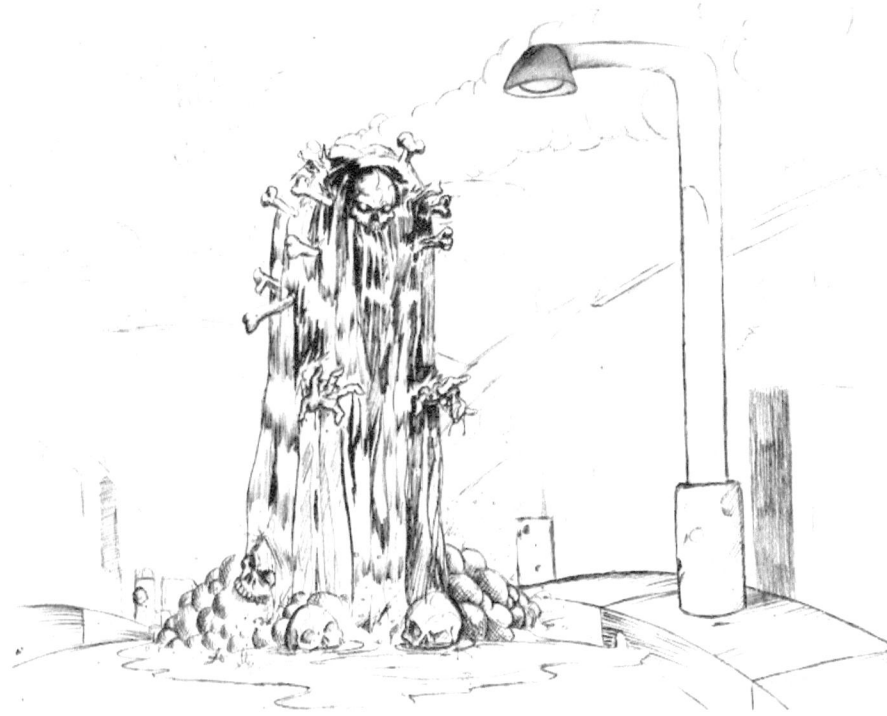

Deathpool roams the streets, sucking up hapless citizens that happen to cross his path. He wanders, always hungry and adding to his death pool. Taking too long in the bath? Deathpool will suck you through the drain. Don't want to get out of the pool? Deathpool will keep you safe in his arms. You like that new waterslide? Slide down into his gaping maw. You like pizza? So does Deathpool.

He's a mystical substance. He is H20. He is rain and mist and cloud. Punch him. Do it. He will suck up your fist and spit out your knuckles, one by one. Deathpool rules.

Skeptic

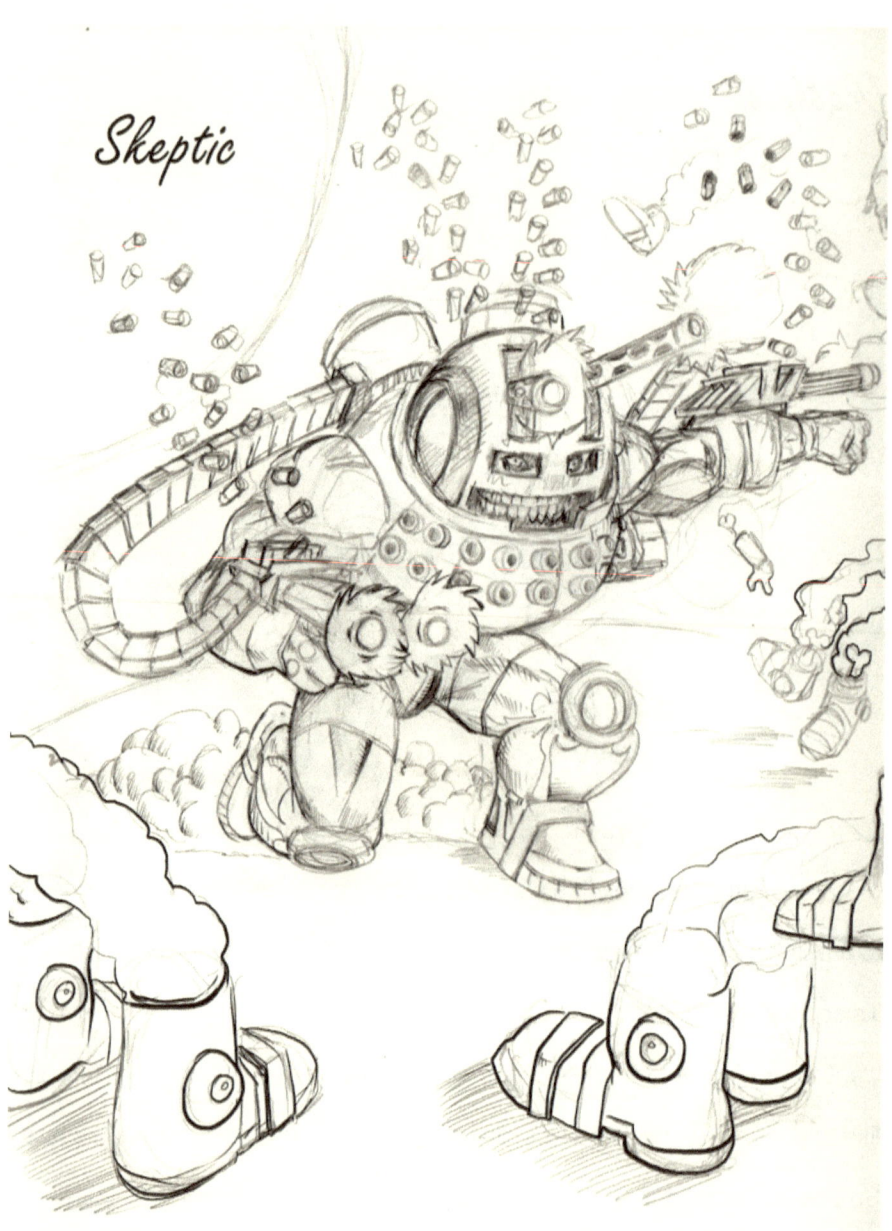

This guy hates everyone and questions everything. Remember when you told your mom you were at school and she didn't believe you? He believes you even less.

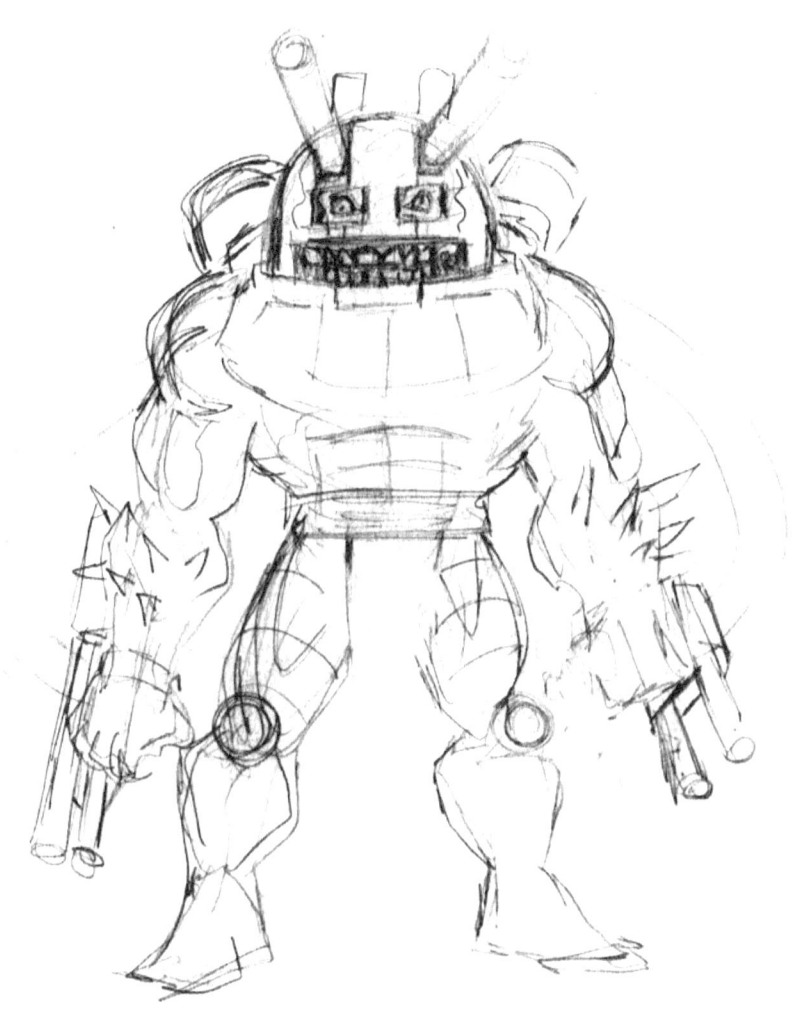

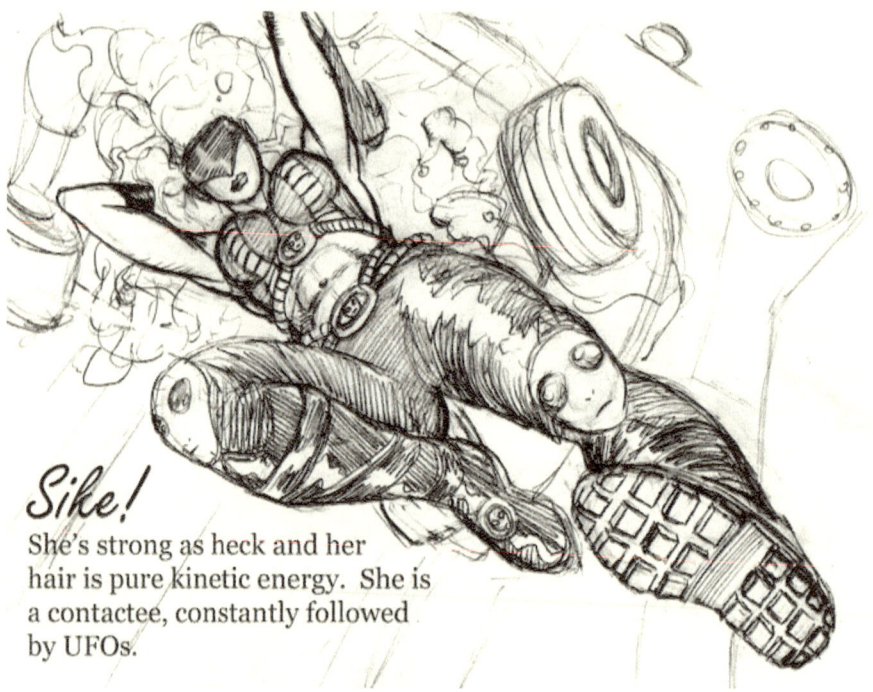

Sike!

She's strong as heck and her hair is pure kinetic energy. She is a contactee, constantly followed by UFOs.

Sike is also an avid jogger. Her favorite TV shows are Ancient Aliens, Jessica Jones, and the Twilight Zone. She covers her eyes because sometimes the kinetic energy bleeds from them. Her kinetic tears can cause permanent eye damage to those who happen to stare at her, so wear safety goggles.

As you can see, she has grey knee pads. She loves the greys, so she likes to rub their faces in the dirt and grime of her adventures. If she happens to accidentally knee you in the face, don't be offended, she must really like you!

Eye-Way

The Eye-Way people are a
strange tribe. They invade other realities
just to make them look better, re-arranging energies
into geometric anomolies. When beings see their work,
they scream, " Eye-Way!"

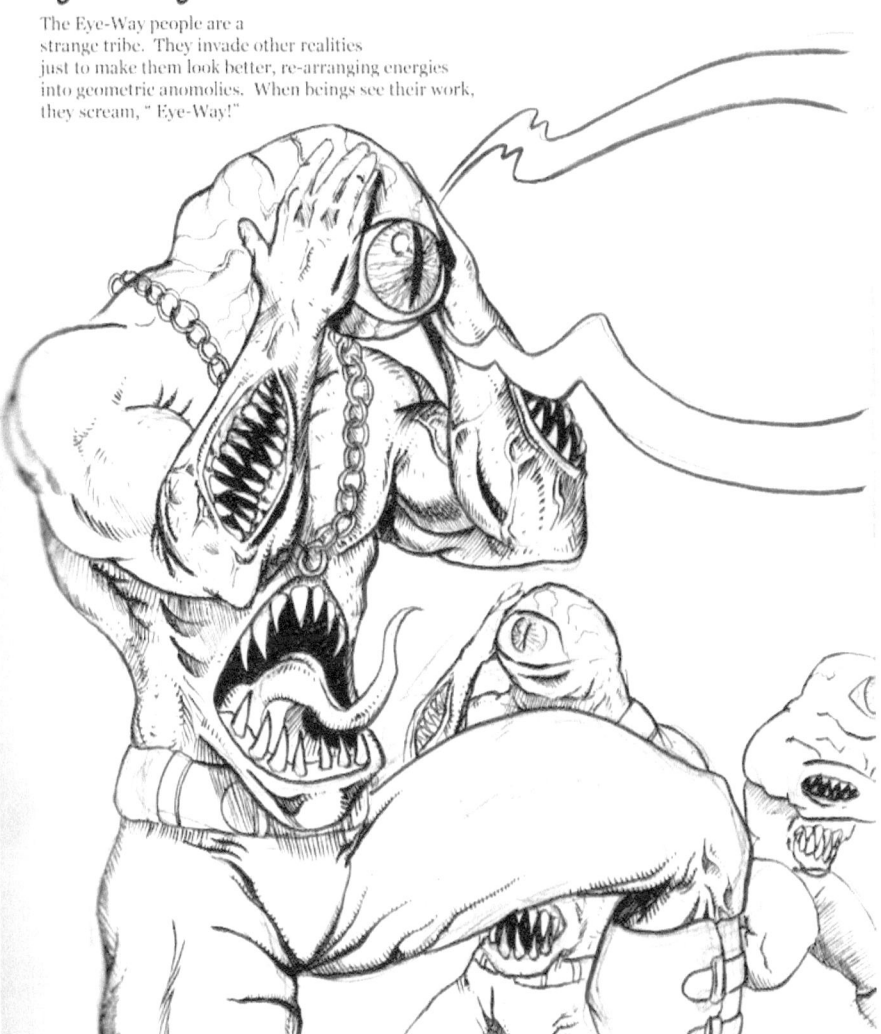

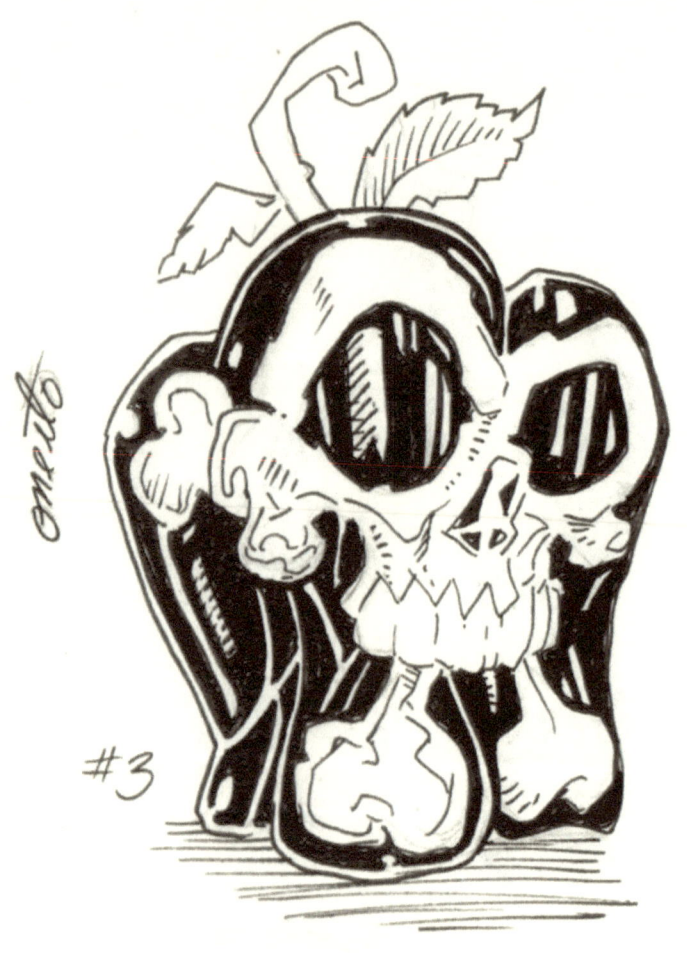

#3

This death apple can cause permanent damage. Just one bite and you're a goner. You can throw it at someone and if you hit them hard enough, they'll explode. Death apples are rare, though, or there would be a lot less of us walking around.

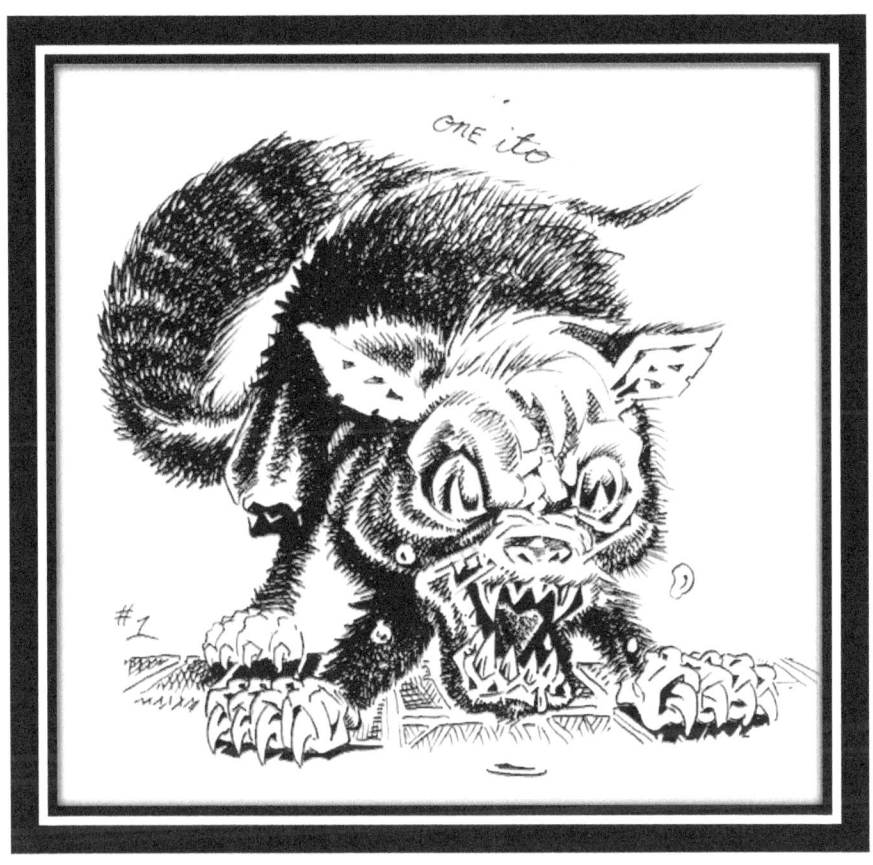

This scary kitty does not like to be carried, pet, or stroked. His fur is not soft, nor smooth: it is prickly, like needles. He doesn't like hugs or warm milk because his first and only owner was a witch. The witch hated everything, and never gave an ounce of love to her cat, making him a spiteful hissing beast. The witch never bothered to name him, but there are those who whisper a terrified wheezing cry as the cat slashes at their throats.

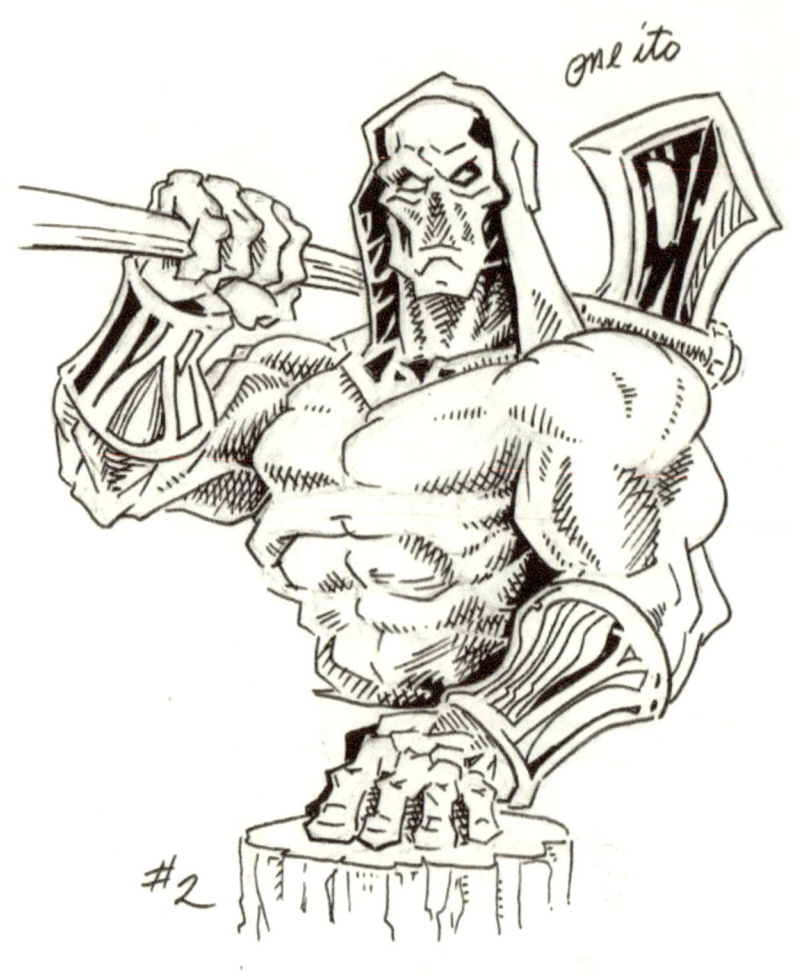

This executioner is a really happy-go-lucky type. He loves his work so much that you can hear him whistling while he swings his ax. As heads roll down the cobblestone streets, he laughs heartily, knowing he will always have work in this town of miscreants.

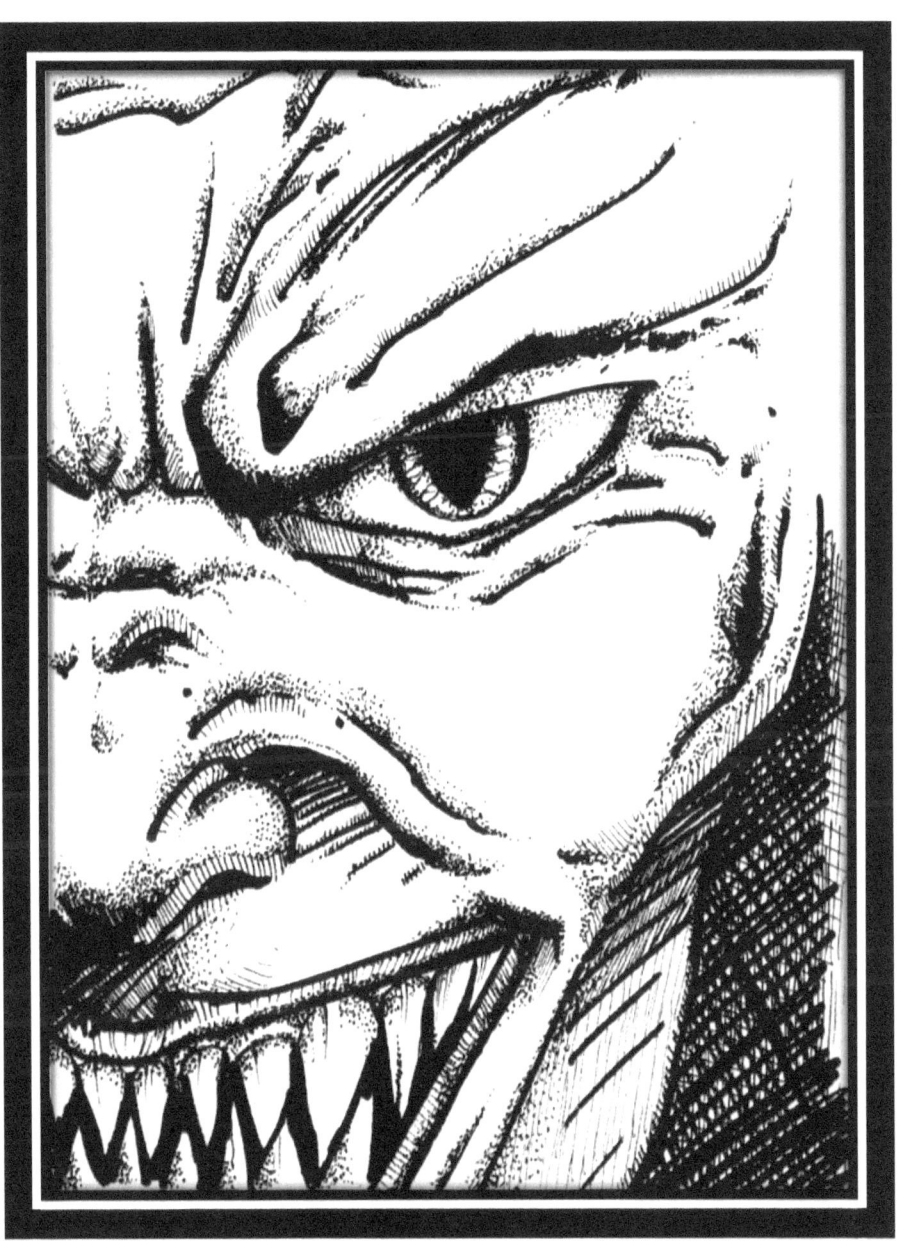

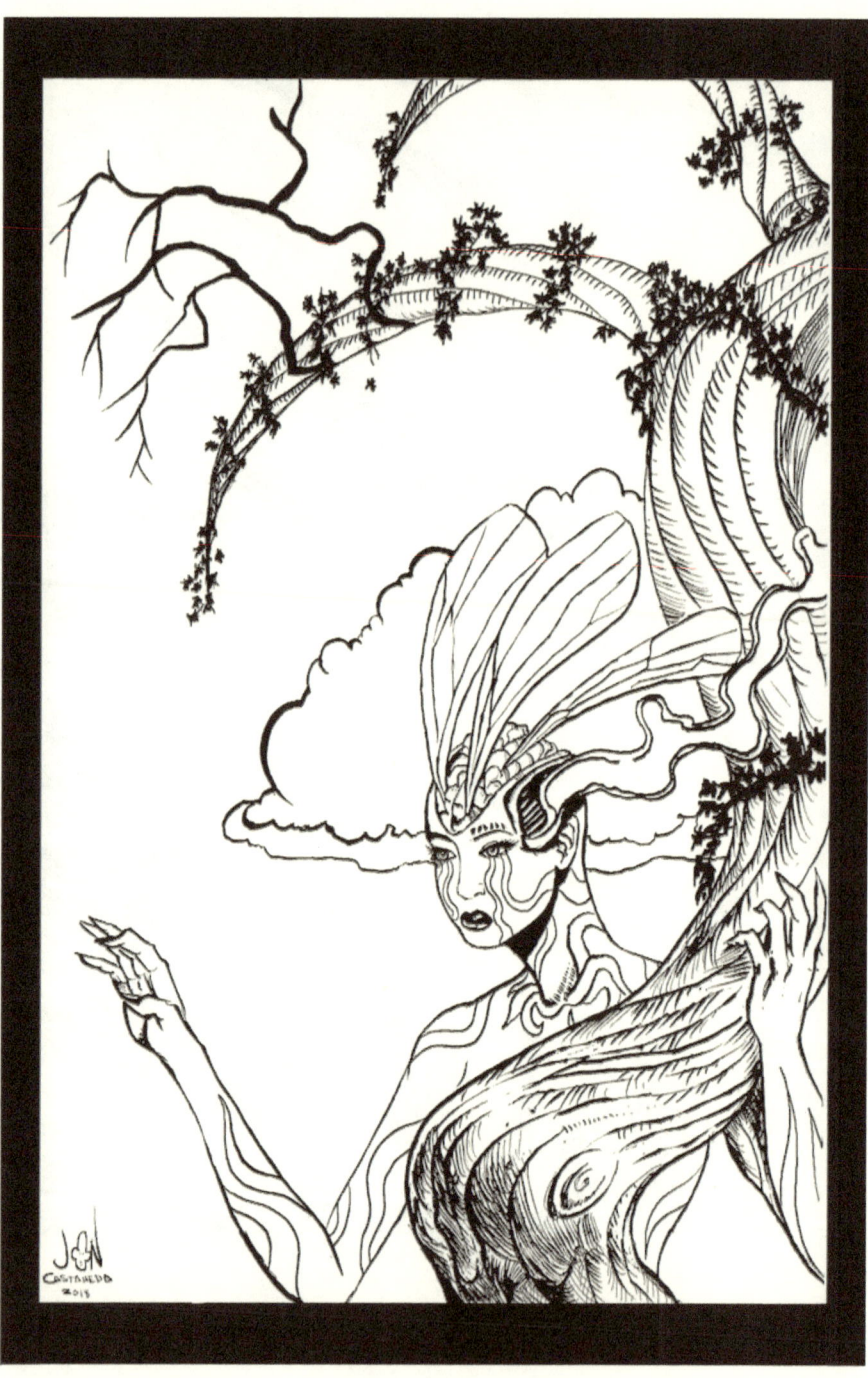

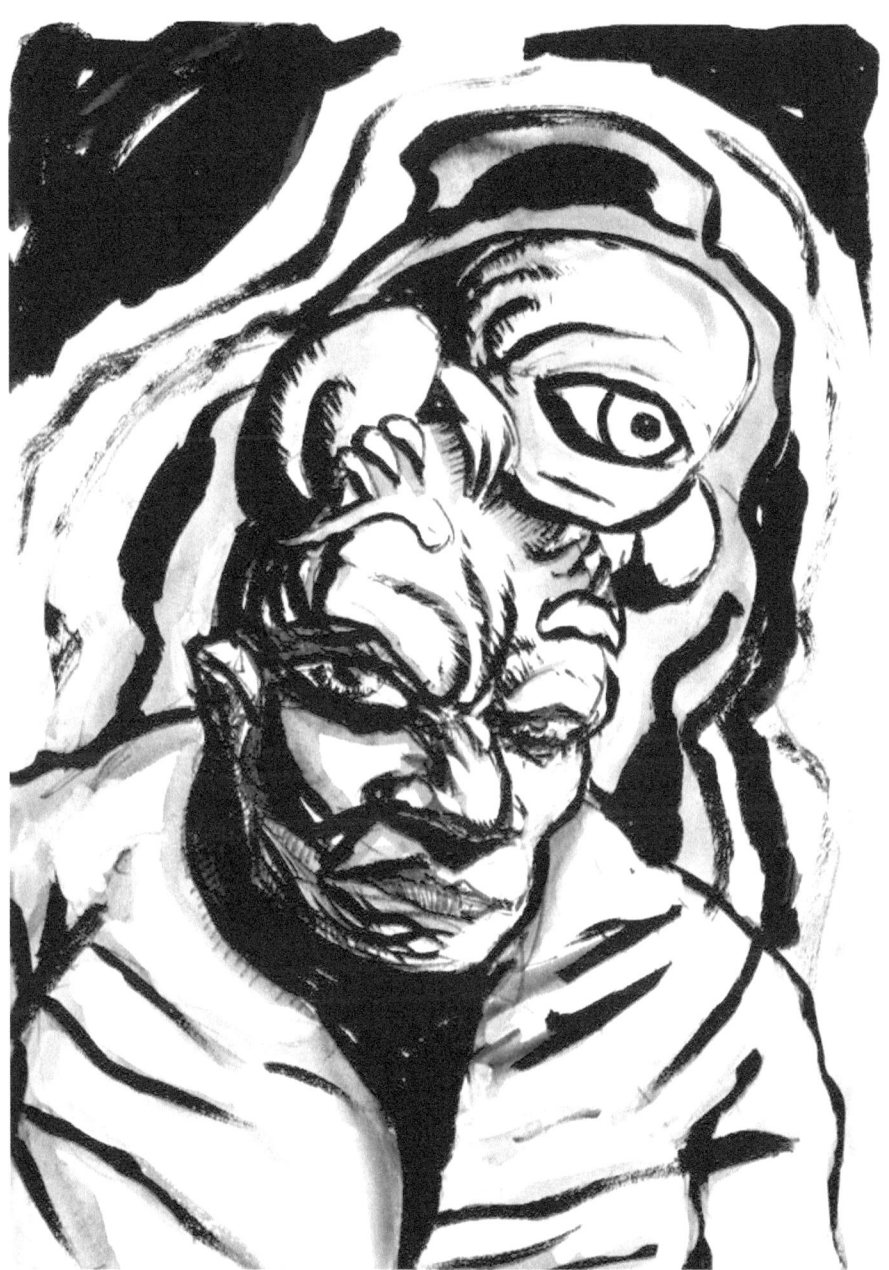

When you wear a cyclopean on your head, things are much clearer. Actually, you can see alternate dimensions. Only others with cyclopeans can detect that you are wearing a cyclopean, for some reason. You'd be surprised how many people have them.

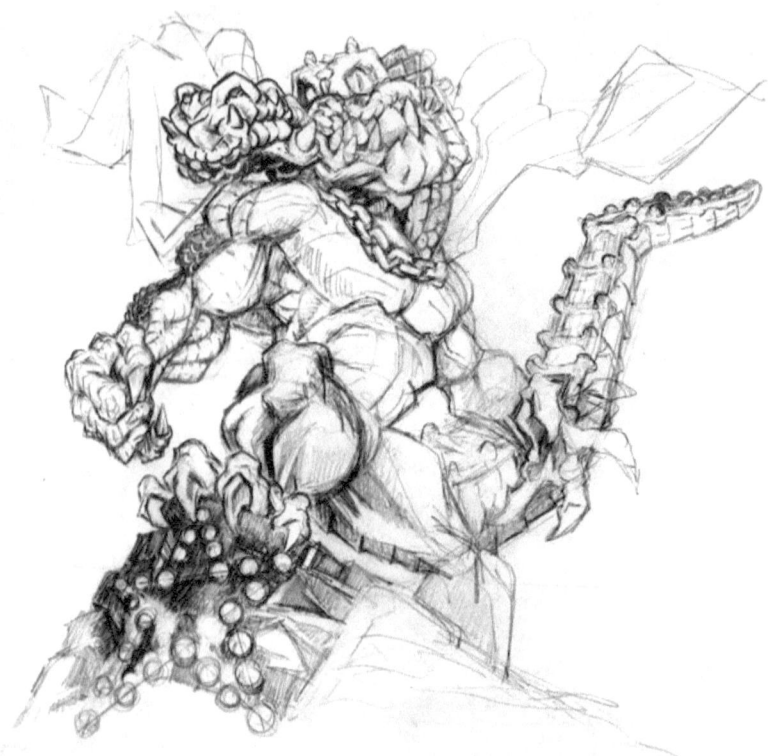

Standing tall atop the Franklins, he scans the scenery, a stoic monumental figure searching for those who would disturb the peace. El Paso is his town, held close to his heart like an old friend, and he'd do anything to save her.

He lurks in the shadows, walking through Segundo Barrio at night, listening for breaking glass, gun shots, or screams. You can find him downtown at the Tap, on the eastside walking down Zaragoza, or on the west side walking up Mesa, always ready to lend a hand to those in danger or in need.

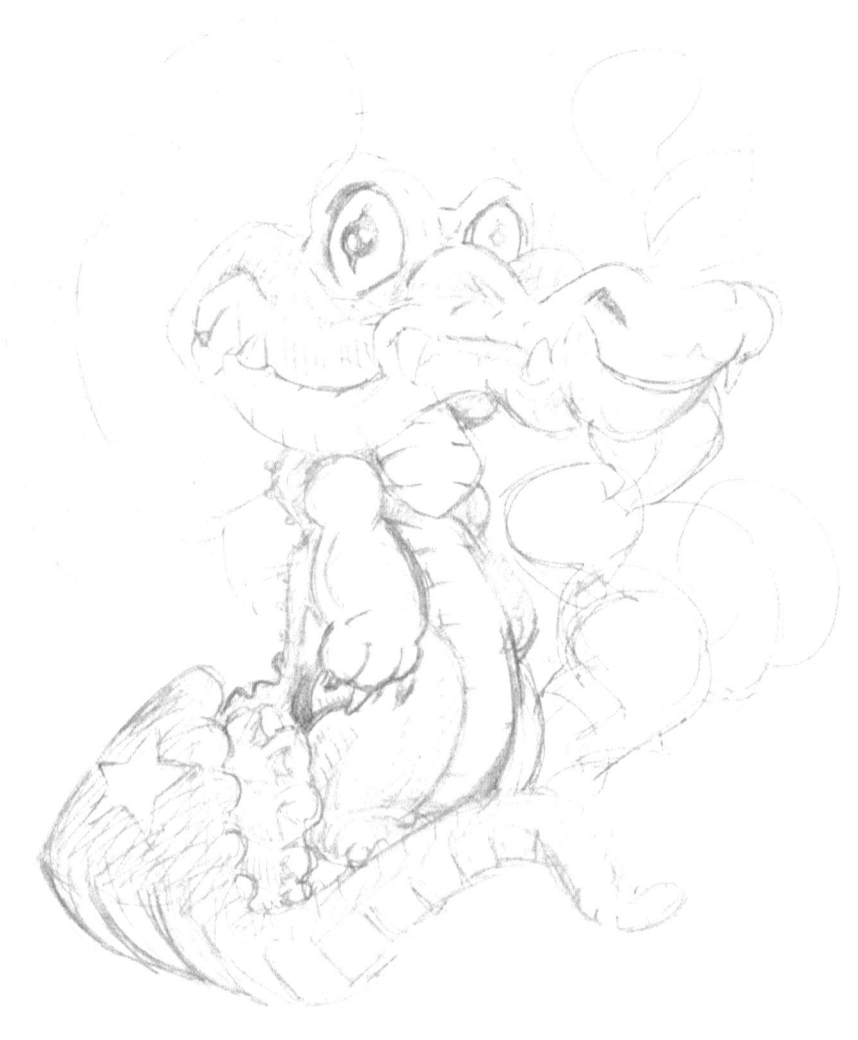

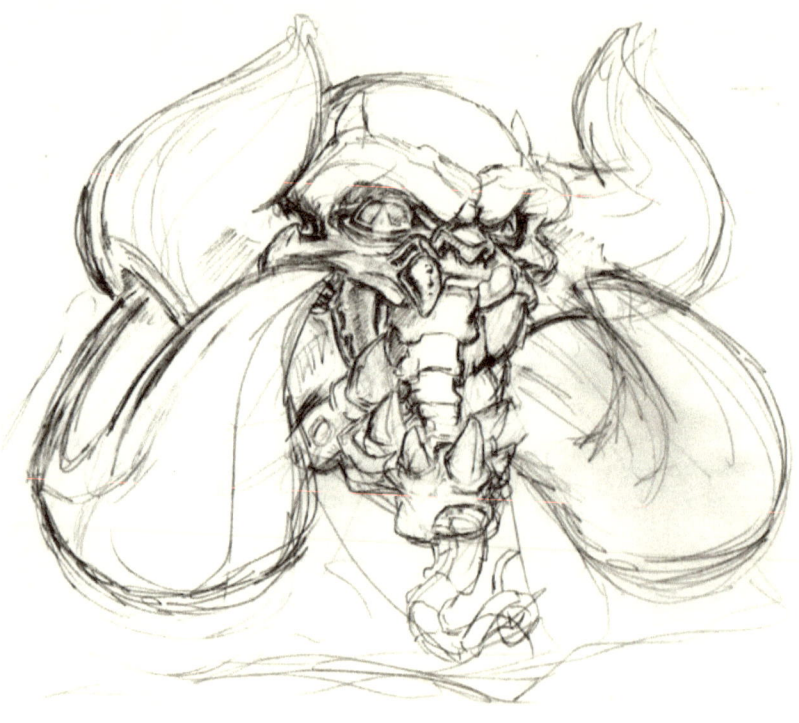

Bull Demons, aka Bloodhorns, appear mostly in South America to shamans of the rain forests. When licking psychedelic frogs, the shamans enter the Bloodhorn's ghostly realm to gain temporary healing and magical powers. Some shamans are able to retrieve Bull Demon skulls from ancient bone yards to use them in battles over spiritual territories.

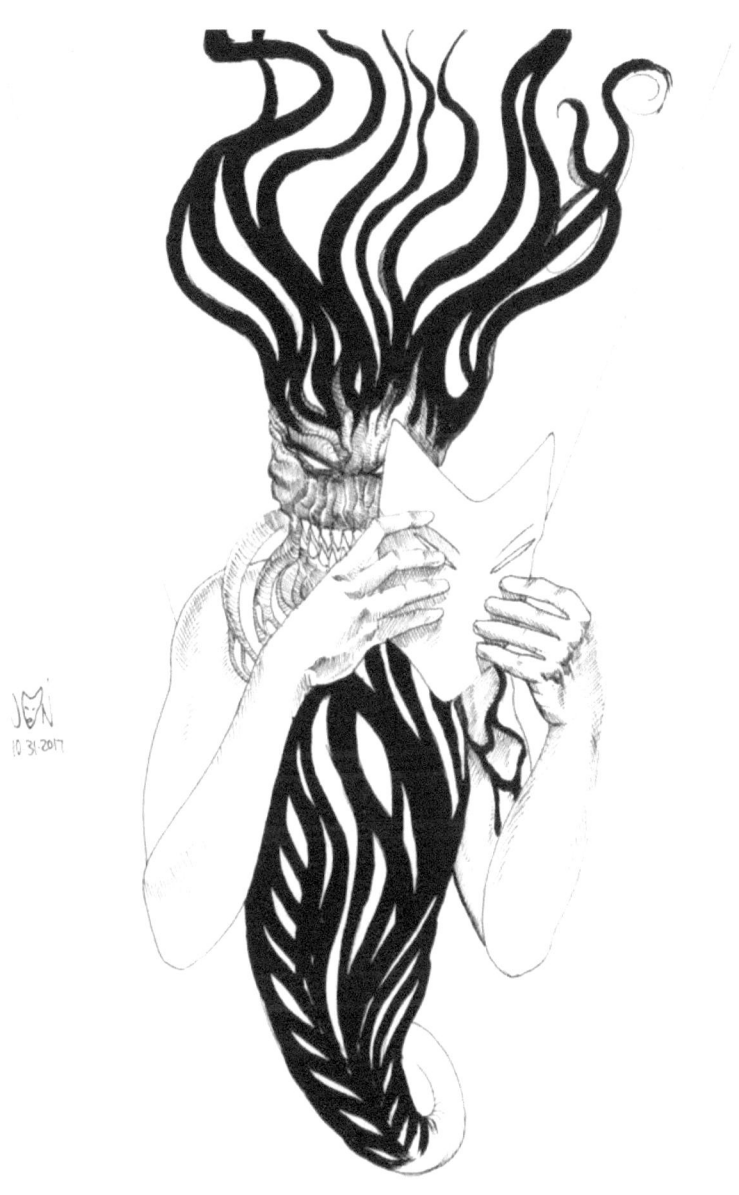

Nemesis is ugly. He is the dark side of One-Eyed Jack, a grey-human hybrid who accidentally gave birth to him through misguided meditation. Nemesis is your fear, your nightmares come to life. He waits to strike as he hides behind a mask. Do you have a Nemesis?

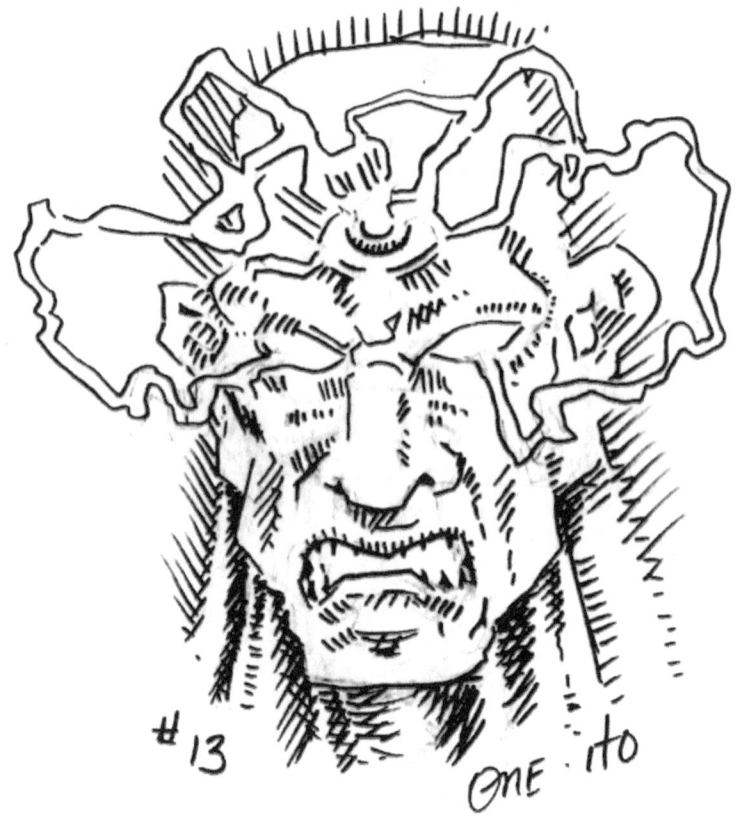

#13 ONE ito

Trips. When he opens his third eye, he trips and goes into other dimensions. He is able to change his frequency to alter his perception and that of beings around him. He can take others into false realities that he creates within his own mind. He zaps back to his true reality when he is able to close his third eye and can leave others in the dream realms.

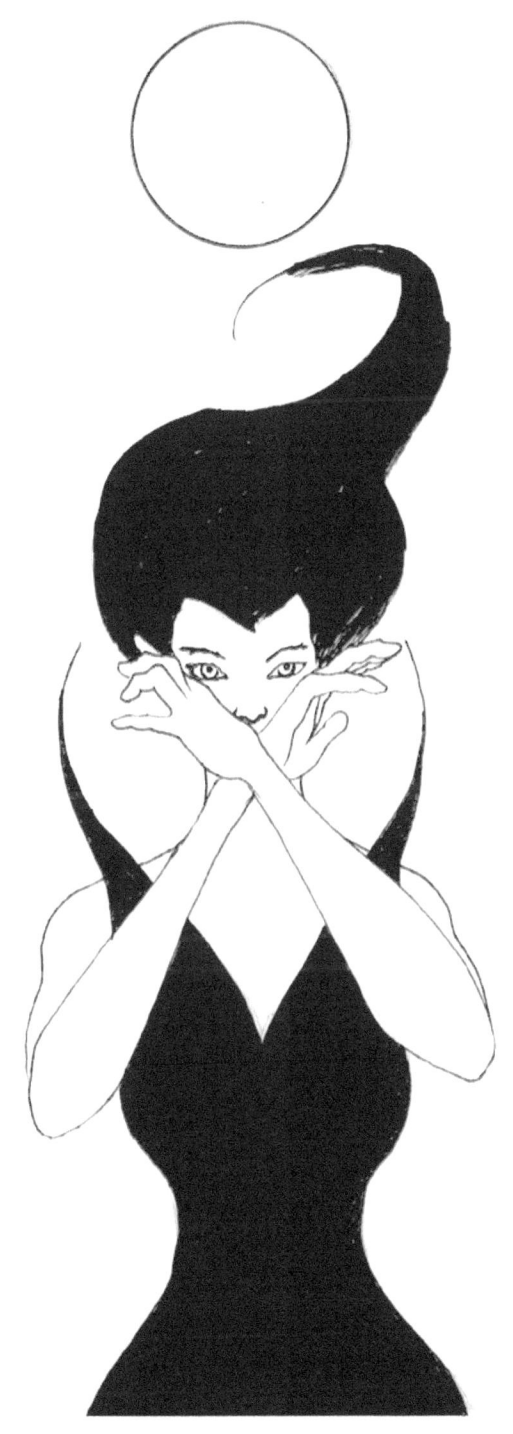

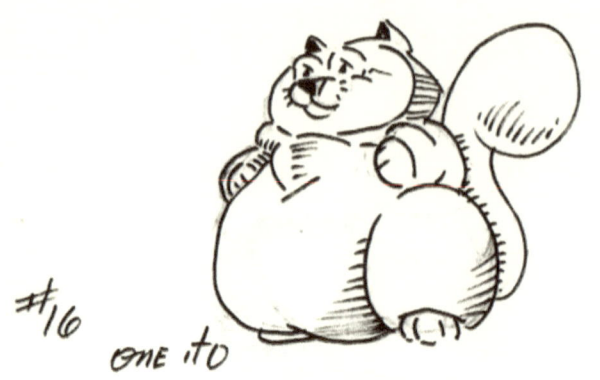

Fat Cat
Fat Cat
Fat Cat
Fat Racoon
Rat Fracoon
Frat movie star
Rocket.

#16

one ito

Mom's so proud. Junior grins wide as his first day of school approaches. He's been dreaming of this day for more than 100 years. Thoughts of smashing and tearing and ripping right through big, fat, juicy books of knowledge run through his head. And that's not the only thing…

#5

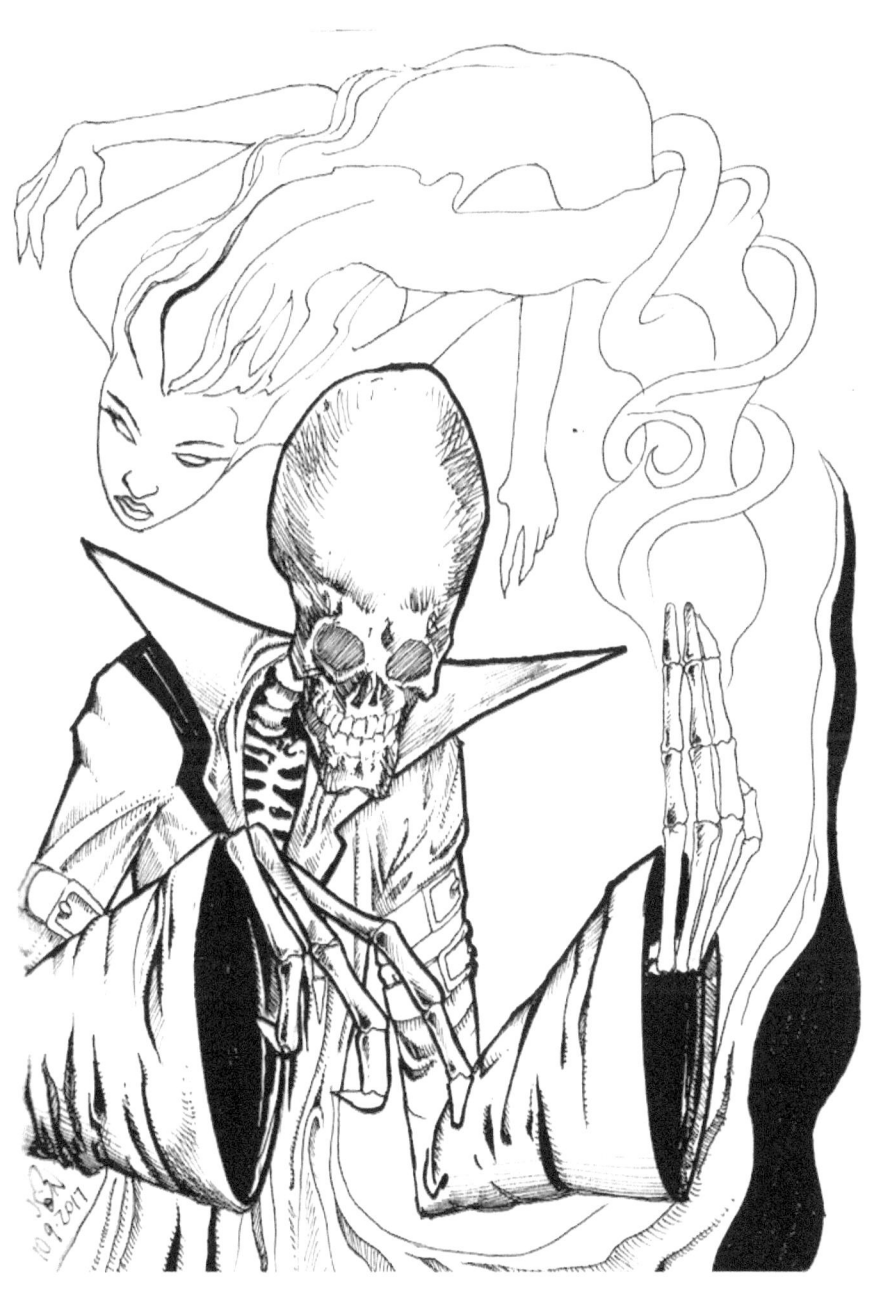

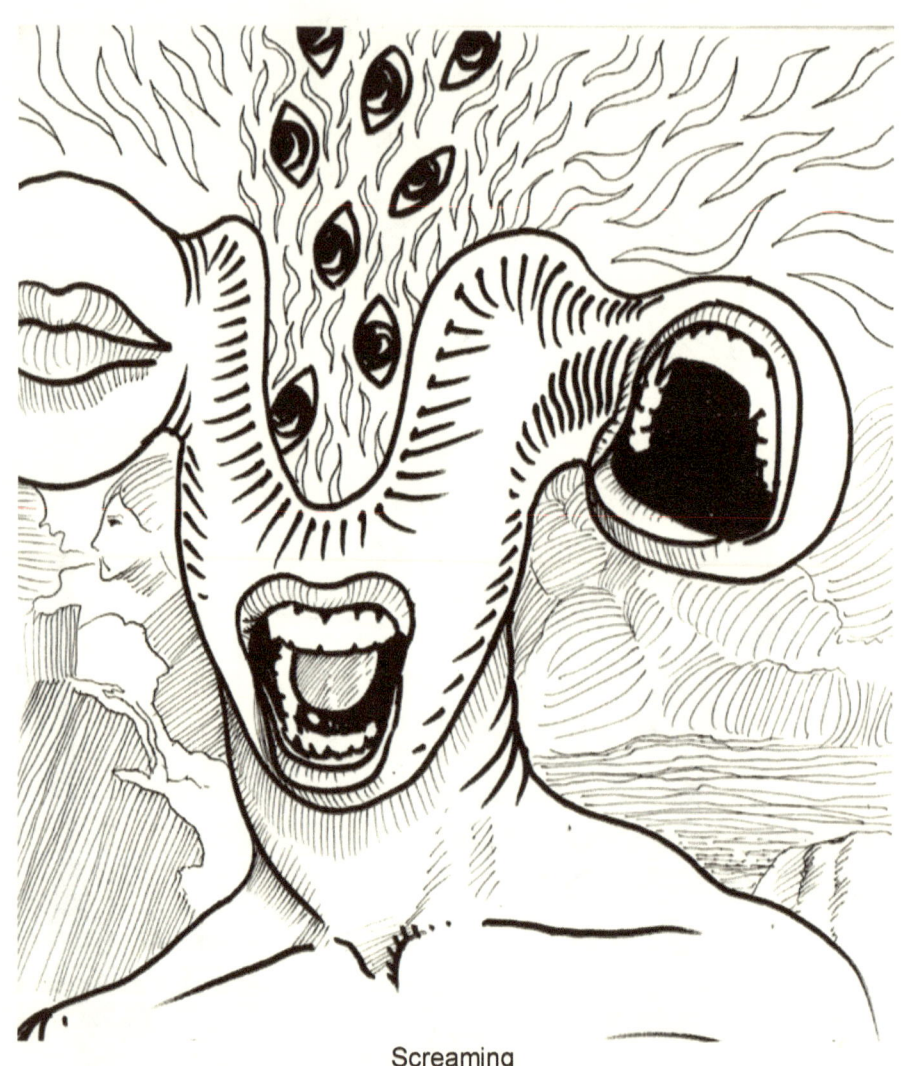

Screaming
And laughing, oh laughing
I saw through, clear glass reality
Still ocean
Crackling fire
A wind that would not cease
Until I was not I
And something other

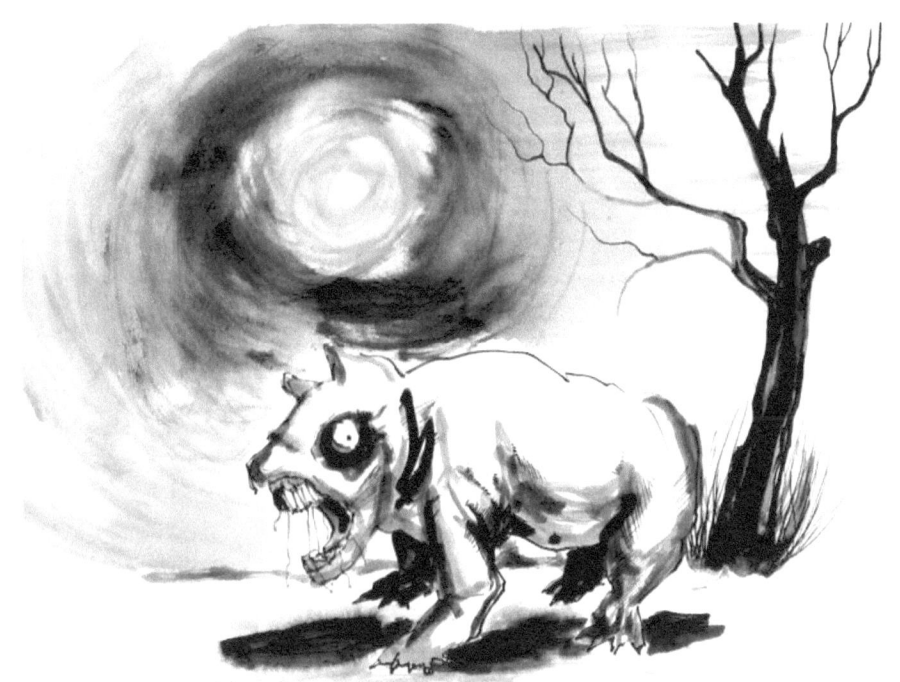

Zombie capybara

Why haunt me with that horrid face

You should not have come back

Your disturbing dance

Causes my eyes to roll back

My spine jerks, reverse spasmolytic

I can almost feel the teeth

Your wheezing decay-breath on my face

Bringing my personal apocalypse

Oh, why do you exist at all?

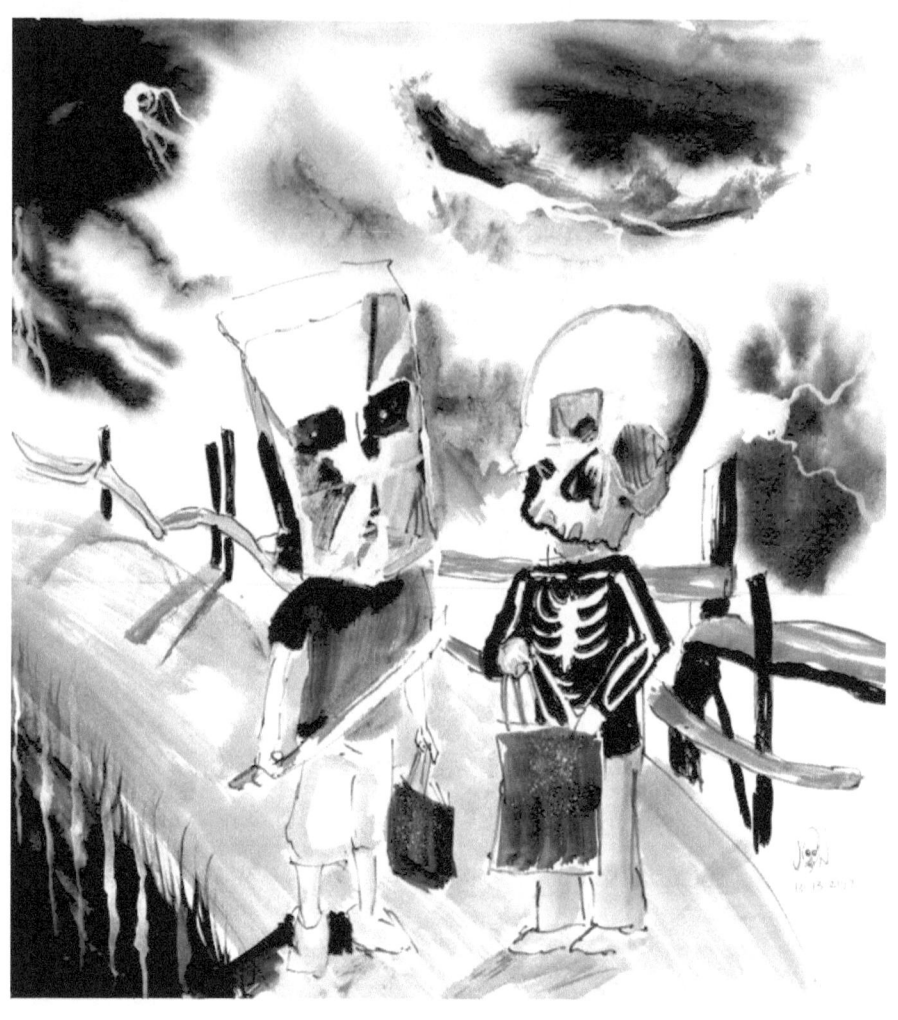

You do not want to meet these guys. Ever. They do not speak, but you can hear their raspy breathing as they approach anyone with candy. It doesn't have to be Halloween. You can be exiting the gas station on a deserted highway and they will be there, off to the side, staring. Throw them some candy... and run!

Pakitusk-Pod
(aka King Tusk)

He's one of a kind! Ol' Tusky was engineered by the US and
North Korea in secret to take out Putin's nuclear subs.

Height: 12 feet
Girth: unknown
Tonnage: unknown
Location: lost at sea.

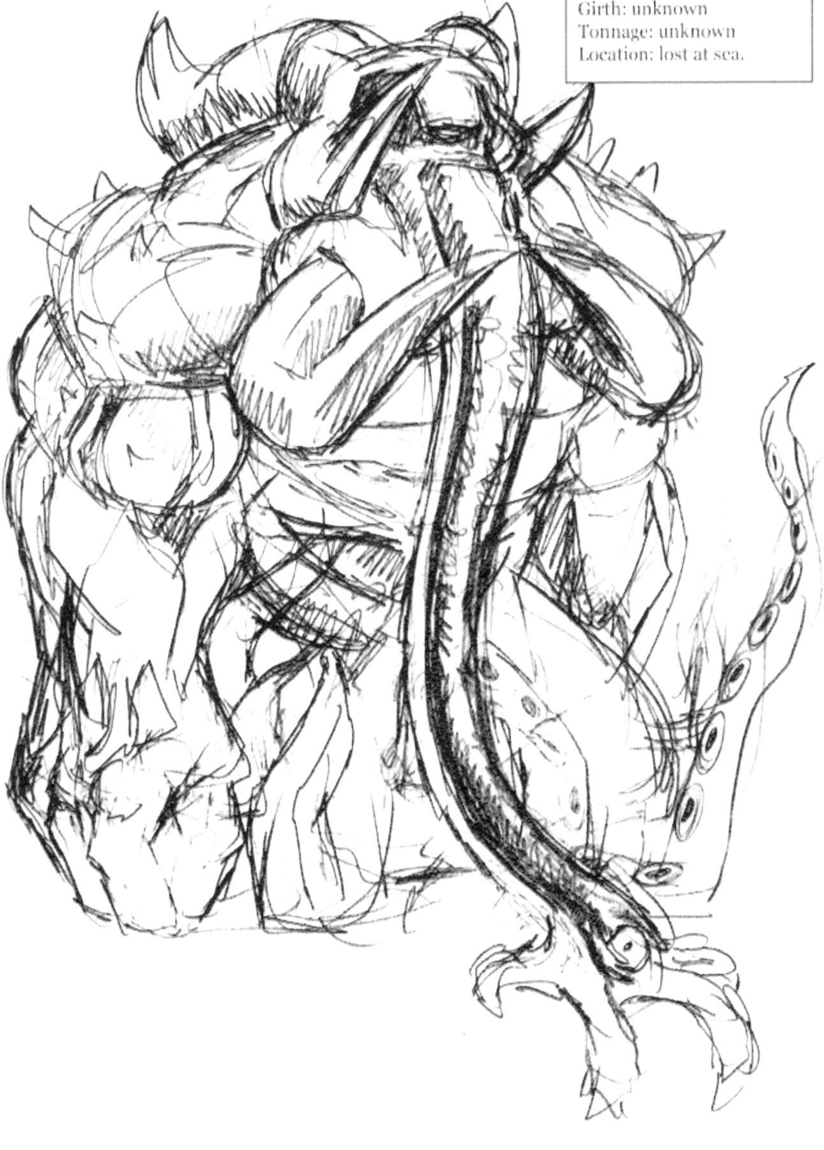

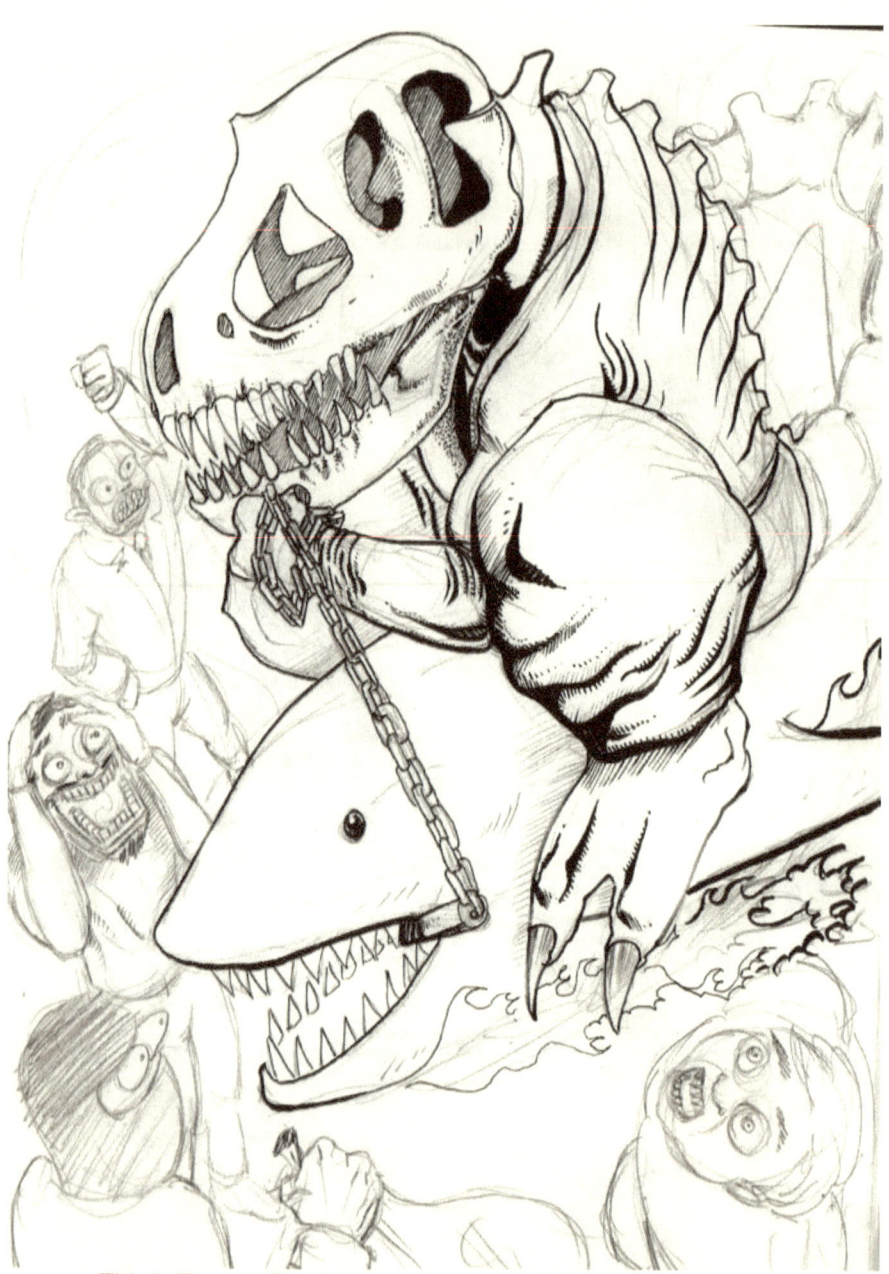

This is Tyrano-Sharkulous. Savior to some, moron to others. He has a very high-pitched voice, sort of like a dolphin.   The shark sounds like your mom eating rice crispies.

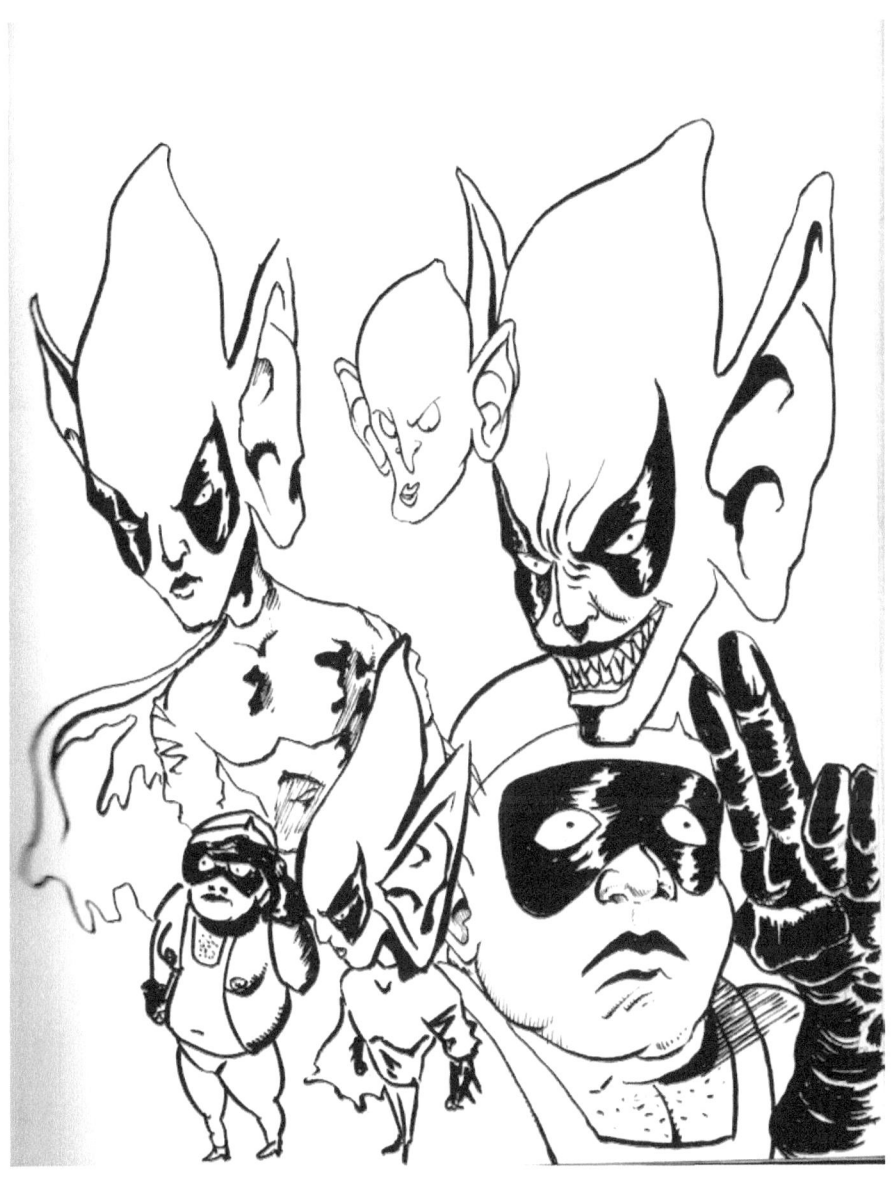

Ricky 'n Sapoman, two more El Paso heroes just trying to make it in the world. If you see them anywhere, compliment Ricky's fat belly and Sapoman's elongated cranium.

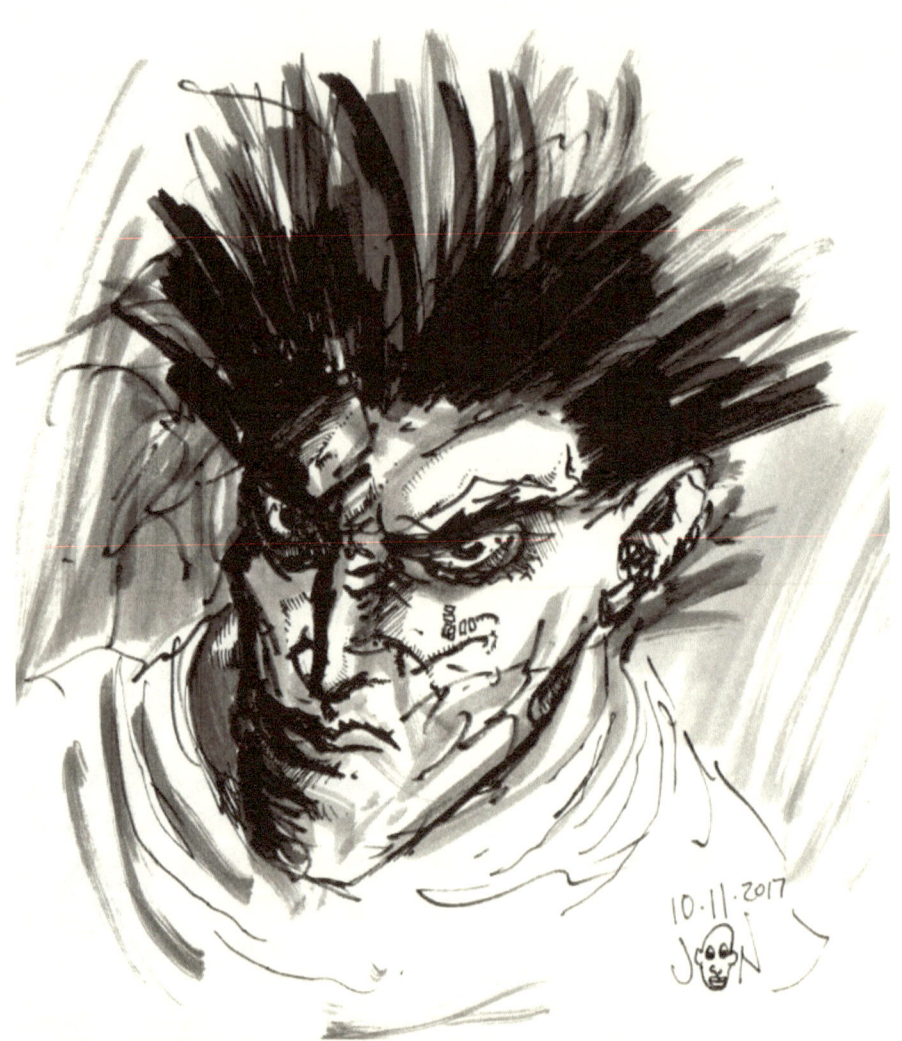

Asylum is his name. He staggers out during the full light of the moon. One glance of his crazed gaze will turn your innards into mush. You will crap your pants. A rash is a terrible thing to have. He knows this. He wills it upon you. Crap your pants, he thinks, and it happens. Run! Run for your life! Save your sanity! Save your pants!

Night-Ray

This is Ray. The night,
illuminated by the great
white disk in the sky, brings
forth this insatiable creature.
As he feasts on your flesh,
he sings delightful
operas.

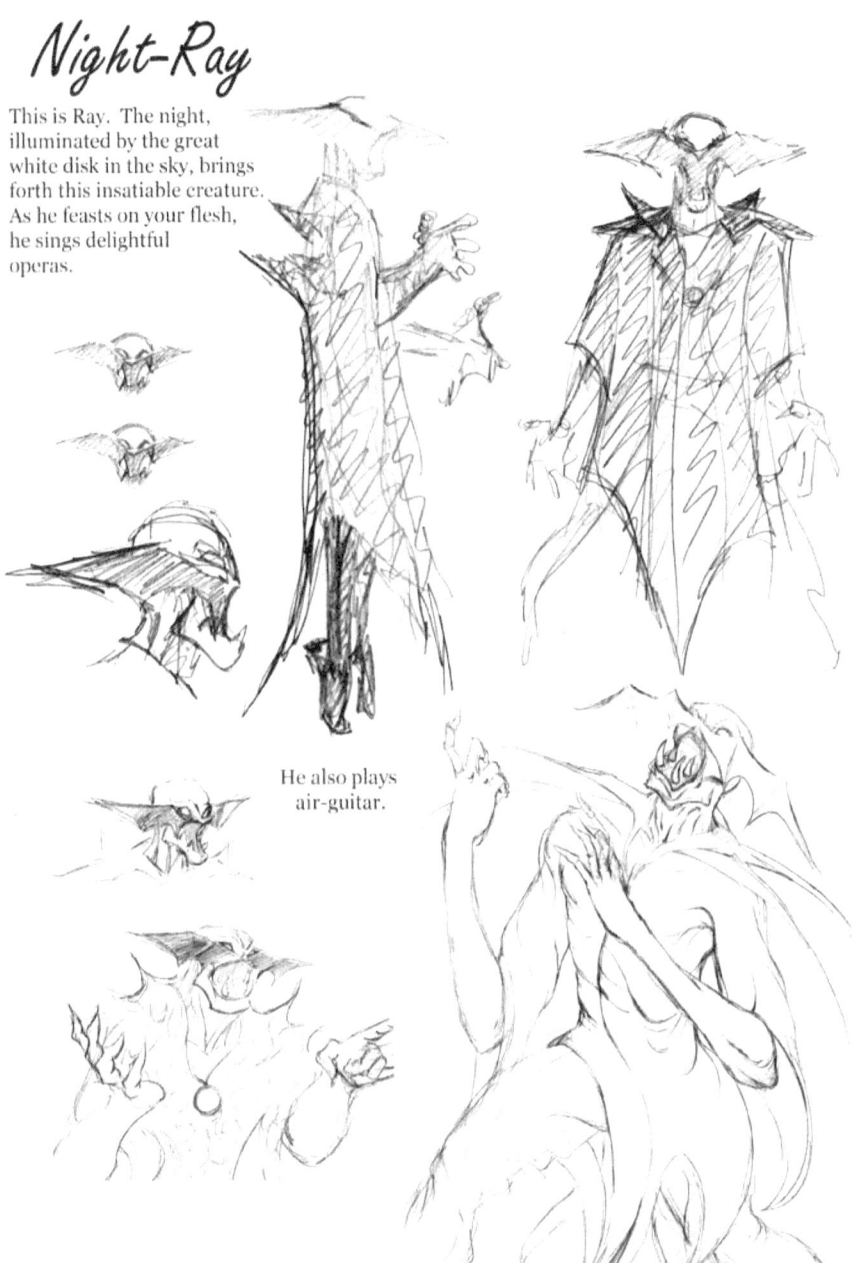

He also plays
air-guitar.